Citizenship

I0502765

Being a Good Citizen

Adrian Vigliano

Heinemann Library
Chicago, Illinois

www.heinemannraintree.com
Visit our website to find out
more information about
Heinemann-Raintree books.

To order:
☎ Phone 888-454-2279
▣ Visit www.heinemannraintree.com
to browse our catalog and order online.

Edited by Rebecca Rissman, Siân Smith, and Charlotte Guillain
Designed by Kimberly Miracle and Steve Mead
Illustrated by Mark Beech
Originated by Capstone Global Library
Printed in the United States of America in North Mankato,
Minnesota. 012013   007138

15 14 13
10 9 8 7 6 5

Library of Congress Cataloging-in-Publication Data

Vigliano, Adrian.
  Being a good citizen / Adrian Vigliano. -- 1st ed.
     p. cm.
  Includes bibliographical references and index.
  ISBN 978-1-4329-3339-5 (hc) -- ISBN 978-1-4329-3340-1
(pb) 1. Citizenship--Juvenile literature. I. Title.
JF801.V55 2008
323.6'5--dc22

                    2008055660

Acknowledgments

We would like to thank Nancy Harris and Adriana Scalise for
their help in the preparation of this book.

Every effort has been made to contact copyright holders of
any material reproduced in this book. Any omissions will
be rectified in subsequent printings if notice is given to the
publisher.

Some words are shown in bold, **like this.** They are explained in "Words to Know" on page 23.

Contents

About this series

Books in the **Citizenship** series introduce readers to character values that embody citizenship. Read this book to encourage children to think of different ways to be a good citizen.

What Is a Citizen?

A **citizen** is a member of a **community**. Communities are made up of the people around us.

There are many ways to be a good citizen. Do you know how to be a good citizen?

At School

When you follow the rules, you help make your school a **fair** place for everyone. How can you follow the rules at school?

You can raise your hand before speaking. You can ask before taking something. You can walk quietly down the hallway. You can wait for the teacher's **instructions**.

A **leader** is someone who takes charge and sets a good example. How can you be a good leader at school?

You can help others with a problem. You can invite others to join in. You can keep trying. You can **praise** others. You can give others a turn to lead.

At Home

When you are helpful, you are thinking of ways to help others. You are also listening to others to learn what they need. How can you be helpful at home?

You can put away toys. You can wash the dishes.
You can help carry things. You can follow
instructions. You can look out for others. You can
ask what you can do to help.

When you are **responsible**, you take charge of what you do. When you are responsible, you do the right thing without being asked to. How can you be responsible?

You can brush your teeth or clean your room without being asked to. You can put on your seatbelt in the car. You can **admit** if you make a mistake.

With Friends

You can be a good **citizen** while you are with friends. You can also be a good citizen by making new friends. Friends **trust** one another and have fun together. How can you make friends?

You can ask someone to play with you. You can **share** your things. You can tell someone you like them. You can listen to others. You can take turns. You can say sorry when you are wrong.

You can be a good friend by being **honest**. When you are honest, you tell the truth and people can **trust** you. How can you be honest with friends?

You can tell someone how you feel. You can return something that is not yours. You can tell someone you made a mistake. You can **admit** that you were wrong.

You can be a good friend by being **fair**. When you are fair, you think of other people and find ways to treat them well. How can you be fair with friends?

You can **share** a snack. You can wait your turn. You can give someone else a turn. You can let others choose what to play. You can think about how others feel.

Being a Good Citizen Every Day

There are many ways to be a good **citizen**.
You can find ways to be a good citizen in
different places.

You can find ways to be a good citizen with different people.

How Can You Be a Good Citizen?

No matter where you are, as a good **citizen** you can be **responsible** for what is going on around you. If you see something that doesn't seem right, you can say something!

You can be a good citizen in your **community** by being a thoughtful family member, student, friend, and neighbor.

You can look for ways to take care of the **environment**.

You can treat other people with kindness and **respect**.

Words to Know

admit	tell something that you may be afraid to tell
citizen	member of the community
community	any group of people. A community can be small like a family, or large like a school.
environment	nature and the world around us
fair	agreeable for everyone
honest	always telling the truth
instruction	written or spoken list of how to do something
leader	someone who takes charge and sets a good example
praise	to tell someone you think they did well
respect	to value something or someone and treat them fairly
responsible	to take charge of yourself and to do the right thing wherever you are
share	to let someone else use what you have; to give someone else a part of what you have
trust	to believe in someone or something

Index

Note to Parents and Teachers

Before Reading:

Tell children that people in a community are called citizens. Communities are made up of the people around us. Ask children if they know how to be good citizens. Create a concept map with the children. In the center of the map write "Good Citizens," and around the center fill in their ideas of how to be a good citizen. Guide them toward words such as *responsible, honest, shares*, and *follows the rules*.

After Reading:

- Assign children a word from a book that relates to being a good citizen. Ask children to write and/or draw a picture that relates to their assigned word. Create a class book from all the work.
- Place children in small groups. Ask each group to create a sign. The sign should show ways to be a good citizen at school. After their posters are complete, walk small groups around the school and help the children to put up their signs.